First Facts®

Snakes

Rattlesnakes

by Joanne Mattern

Consultant:
Robert T. Mason, PhD
Professor of Zoology
J.C. Braly Curator of Vertebrates
Oregon State University, Corvallis

press®

Mankato, Minnesota

First Facts is published by Capstone Press,
151 Good Counsel Drive, P.O. Box 669, Mankato, Minnesota 56002.
www.capstonepress.com

Library of Congress Cataloging-in-Publication Data
Mattern, Joanne, 1963–
    Rattlesnakes / by Joanne Mattern.
    p. cm. — (First facts. Snakes)
    Includes bibliographical references and index.
    Summary: "A brief introduction to rattlesnakes, including their habitat, food, and
life cycle" — Provided by publisher.
    ISBN-13: 978-1-4296-1926-4 (hardcover)
    ISBN-10: 1-4296-1926-0 (hardcover)
    1. Rattlesnakes — Juvenile literature. I. Title. II. Series.
QL666.O69M358 2009
597.96'38 — dc22
                                                      2007051902

Editorial Credits

Lori Shores, editor; Ted Williams, designer and illustrator; Danielle Ceminsky, illustrator;
    Jo Miller, photo researcher

Photo Credits

Alamy/Arco Images, cover
Art Life Images/age fotostock/John Cancalosi, 18
Corbis/Joe McDonald, 13
Dreamstime/Dndavis, 9
Getty Images Inc./National Geographic/Bianca Lavies, 17; Joel Sartore, 14–15
iStockphoto/sonya greer, 5
Nature Picture Library/John Cancalosi, 11
Pete Carmichael, 21
Place Stock Photo/Bruce Farnsworth, 6
Shutterstock/John Bell, 1; Nahimoff, background texture (throughout); Rusty Dodson, 20
Visuals Unlimited/Michael Redmer, 8

Essential content terms are **bold** and are defined at the bottom of the page where they first appear.

1 2 3 4 5 6 13 12 11 10 09 08

Table of Contents

A Noisy Snake

Say hello to a snake that really makes some noise! The rattlesnake gets its name from its special tail. The end of its tail has hard rings. Together these rings are called a rattle. When the snake shakes its tail, the rattle makes a loud buzzing noise.

Fun Fact!

Some people say a rattlesnake sounds like leaves rustling or the buzzing of an insect.

rattle

5

scales

What's That Sound?

A rattlesnake's rattle is made of rings of hard skin. When the rings rub together, the rattle makes noise.

Why do rattlesnakes shake their tails? The rattle sound is a warning that the snake is ready to attack. When an animal hears the rattle, it knows it had better run!

Fun Fact!

To make the rattle sound, the snake moves its tail very fast. The rattle moves back and forth more than 60 times each second!

ridgenosed rattlesnake

Long and Longer

The shortest rattlesnake is the ridgenosed rattlesnake. It is just 1 foot (0.3 meters) long. This snake weighs only about 4 ounces (113 grams).

The longest rattlesnake is the eastern diamondback. It can grow up to 8 feet (2.4 meters) long. Most diamondbacks weigh between 4 and 10 pounds (1.8 to 4.5 kilograms).

eastern diamondback

Where in the World?

Many rattlesnakes live in the western part of the United States. Most live in the hot, dry desert. Some rattlesnakes live high in mountains.

Rattlesnake Range

☐ where rattlesnakes live

North America

South America

Europe

Africa

Asia

Australia

Antarctica

N
W E
S

Rattlesnakes are not active in cold weather. That's because snakes are **cold-blooded** reptiles. When the weather gets too cold, they **hibernate**.

cold-blooded: having body temperature that changes with surroundings
hibernate: to spend the winter in a resting state

A Whole New Skin

Snakes are covered with pieces of hard, dry skin called scales. As a snake grows, it **sheds** its skin and grows a new one. Shedding is important for a rattlesnake. When a rattlesnake sheds, a piece of old skin stays on its tail. This piece becomes part of the rattle.

Fun Fact!

Snakes shed their skin in one whole piece. Other reptiles can't do that.

shed: to let something fall or drop off

shed skin

Fangs and Venom

Rattlesnakes have two long, curved teeth called fangs. The fangs are connected to glands that produce **venom**. When the snake bites, venom flows through the fangs. The venom quickly kills the unlucky animal.

Fun Fact!

Rattlesnake venom is strong enough to kill a person. But with medical treatment, most cases of snakebite are not fatal.

venom: a harmful liquid

What's for Dinner?

Rattlesnakes usually eat mice, rats, and lizards. They wait for an animal to come near and then bite it. But the bite doesn't kill the **prey** right away.

After a rattlesnake bites its prey, it quickly lets go. The animal runs away, but it doesn't get far. The prey soon dies from the rattlesnake's venom. Then the snake follows the prey and eats it.

Fun Fact!

A rattlesnake swallows its prey whole. After a big meal, the snake won't eat for several weeks.

prey: an animal that is hunted by another animal for food

Life Cycle of a Rattlesnake

Newborn

Between four and 30 baby snakes are born at one time.

Young

Young rattlesnakes eat lizards and other small prey.

Adult

Rattlesnakes are ready to mate in three years.

Brood

Growing Up

Rattlesnakes do not lay eggs like some other reptiles. Three months after mating, a female rattlesnake gives birth to a **brood** of live snakes.

Baby rattlesnakes can hunt from the time they are born. Rattlesnake mothers only stay near their babies for a few days. Then the young snakes are on their own.

Fun Fact!
A baby rattlesnake's venom is as strong as an adult snake's. They just don't have as much.

brood: a group of animals born at one time

Baby's First Rattle

A newborn rattlesnake sheds its skin after a week or two. This makes the first part of the rattle. When it sheds again, it will have two pieces to rattle together.

Amazing but True!

Everyone knows you can milk a cow. But you can also milk a snake! Scientists take the venom from a rattlesnake's fangs. They hold the snake's head and let the venom flow into a cup. The venom is then used to make medicine for snakebites.

Glossary

brood (BROOHD) — a group of young animals born at the same time

cold-blooded (KOLD-BLUH-id) — having a body temperature that changes with the surroundings

hibernate (HYE-bur-nate) — to spend winter in a resting state as if in a deep sleep

prey (PRAY) — an animal hunted by another animal for food

shed (SHED) — to let something fall or drop off; reptiles shed their skin.

venom (VEN-uhm) — a harmful liquid produced by some animals

Read More

Lockwood, Sophie. *Rattlesnakes.* World of Reptiles. Chanhassen, Minn.: Child's World, 2006.

Murray, Julie. *Rattlesnakes.* Animal Kingdom. Edina, Minn.: Abdo, 2005.

O'Hare, Ted. *Rattlesnakes.* Amazing Snakes. Vero Beach, Fla.: Rourke, 2005.

Internet Sites

FactHound offers a safe, fun way to find Internet sites related to this book. All of the sites on FactHound have been researched by our staff.

Here's how:
1. Visit *www.facthound.com*
2. Choose your grade level.
3. Type in this book ID **1429619260** for age-appropriate sites. You may also browse subjects by clicking on letters, or by clicking on pictures and words.
4. Click on the **Fetch It** button.

FactHound will fetch the best sites for you!

Index